**For Mark Morelli—J.W.**

**For my uncles Vitor and Luís—A.C.**

**For the record:** Though not exactly a fan of publicity these days, Sandy Koufax is very much alive and well and living in Florida. In the recent past, he sometimes dropped by Dodgertown, the Los Angeles Dodgers' spring training camp (since relocated to Arizona), to offer helpful hints to young pitchers.

Published by Schwartz & Wade Books
an imprint of Random House Children's Books
a division of Random House, Inc., New York

Text copyright © 2009 by Jonah Winter
Illustrations copyright © 2009 by André Carrilho

Visit us on the Web! www.randomhouse.com/kids
Educators and librarians, for a variety of teaching tools, visit us at www.randomhouse.com/teachers

*Library of Congress Cataloging-in-Publication Data*
Winter, Jonah.
You Never Heard of Sandy Koufax?! / by Jonah Winter ; illustrated by André Carrilho.
 p. cm.
ISBN 978-0-375-83738-8 (trade)
ISBN 978-0-375-93738-5 (lib. bdg.)
1. Koufax, Sandy, 1935– —Juvenile literature.
2. Baseball players—United States—Biography—Juvenile literature.
3. Los Angeles Dodgers (Baseball team)—Biography—Juvenile literature.
I. Carrilho, André. II. Title.
GV865.K67W56 2009
796.357092—dc22
[B]
 2007041860

The text of this book is set in Fairplex and Franklin Gothic.
The illustrations are rendered in graphite on paper, with color and texture added using Adobe Photoshop.
Book design by Rachael Cole

MANUFACTURED IN CHINA
10 9 8 7 6 5 4 3 2 1
First Edition

About the cover: This lenticular cover was created using a plastic sheet composed of a series of tightly spaced, curved ridges. Each ridge is a tiny lens, called a lenticule. André Carrilho rendered three images, which were digitally sliced into strips and printed on this plastic sheet, with one strip from each image behind each lenticule. The lenses let you see only one set of strips at a time, creating the illusion of movement as you turn the cover.

# YOU NEVER HEARD OF
# SANDY KOUFAX?!

by **JONAH WINTER**
illustrations by **ANDRÉ CARRILHO**

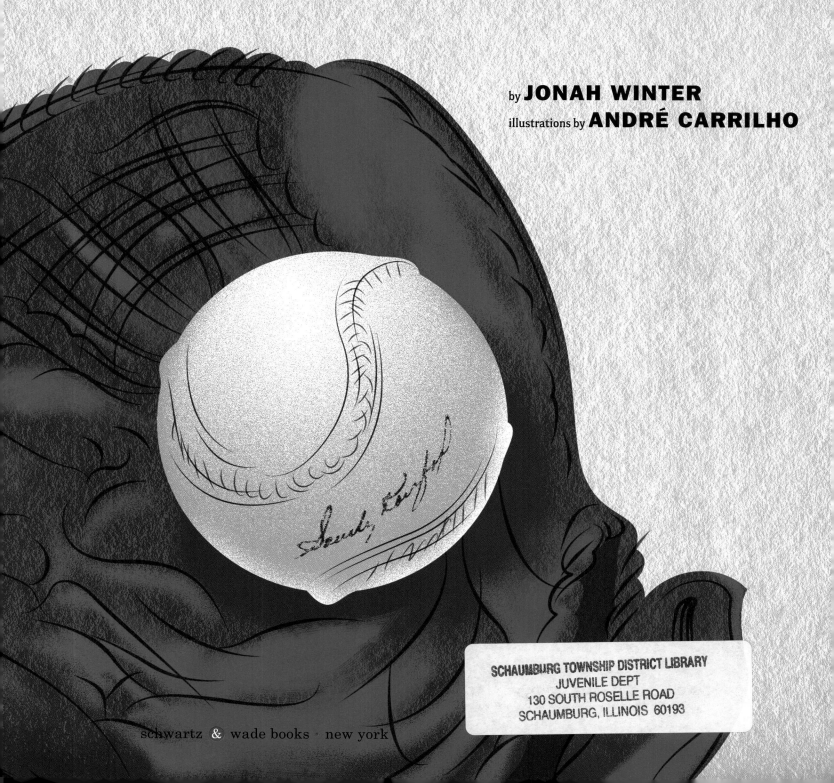

schwartz & wade books · new york

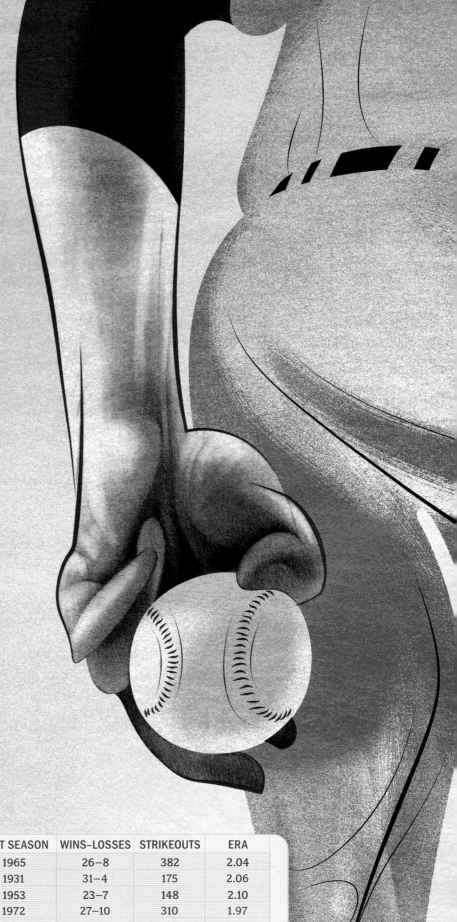

| BEST LEFTIES OF ALL TIME | BEST SEASON | WINS–LOSSES | STRIKEOUTS | ERA |
|---|---|---|---|---|
| Sandy Koufax | 1965 | 26–8 | 382 | 2.04 |
| Lefty Grove | 1931 | 31–4 | 175 | 2.06 |
| Warren Spahn | 1953 | 23–7 | 148 | 2.10 |
| Steve Carlton | 1972 | 27–10 | 310 | 1.97 |
| Randy Johnson | 2002 | 24–5 | 334 | 2.32 |

**Y**ou gotta be kidding! You never heard of *Sandy Koufax*?! He was only the greatest lefty who ever pitched in the game of baseball.

Well, for six years he was, anyway. From 1961 to 1966, almost no one could hit the guy. The mighty Mickey Mantle, one of the greatest power hitters of all time: *whiff!* After the Mick struck out one day, he turned to the catcher and said, "What the heck was **THAT?**"

The walloping Willie Stargell, who slammed 475 homers: *whiff!* "Hittin' a Koufax fastball," Willie said, "was like tryin' to drink coffee with a fork."

Even Willie Mays, maybe the greatest all-around player in the history of the majors: *whiff!*

For six years, Koufax stood on the pitcher's mound like a prince, and when you looked at that serious mug of his, you could tell he was gonna beat you.

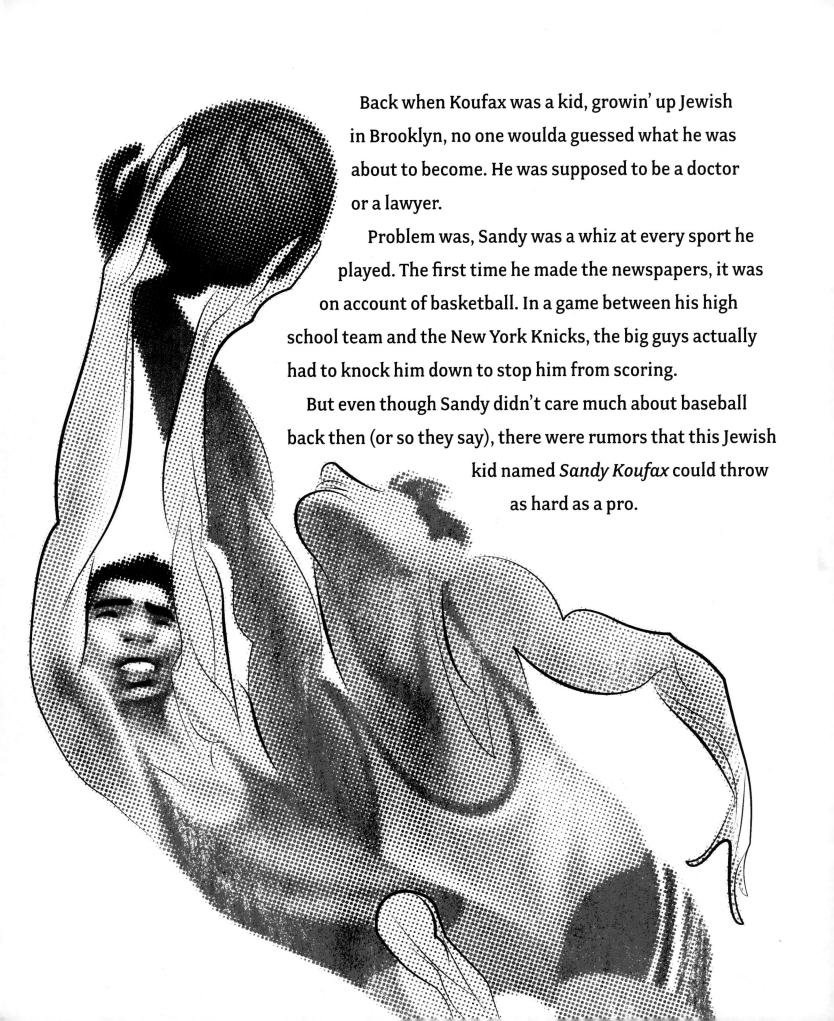

Back when Koufax was a kid, growin' up Jewish in Brooklyn, no one woulda guessed what he was about to become. He was supposed to be a doctor or a lawyer.

Problem was, Sandy was a whiz at every sport he played. The first time he made the newspapers, it was on account of basketball. In a game between his high school team and the New York Knicks, the big guys actually had to knock him down to stop him from scoring.

But even though Sandy didn't care much about baseball back then (or so they say), there were rumors that this Jewish kid named *Sandy Koufax* could throw as hard as a pro.

It didn't take long for the major league scouts to start sniffin' around Dyker Field, where Sandy was pitchin' to his pals in sandlot games.

One day one of our scouts, Al Campanis, invites Sandy to Ebbets Field—
home of our team, the Brooklyn Dodgers—so's he can see the hotshot
pitch. After battin' *just one time* against him, Campanis has seen enough.
He says to Sandy, "Kid, how'd you like to play for us? Don't think too hard."

Quick as you can say "Jackie Robinson," this nineteen-year-old squirt was wearin' Dodgers blue and earnin' more dough than some of us old-timers.

Turns out Sandy earned most of it just warmin' the bench. See, he was new, a rookie . . . and rookies are known to lose a lot. It was 1955, and the Dodgers had a shot to win the pennant. The kid was too big a risk.

And most every time our manager, Alston, did let Sandy pitch, the rookie was unpredictable—all over the map. He could throw strikes, but mostly he was nowhere near the strike zone. We could tell he was throwin' too hard. And when you overthrow, you lose control. And when you lose control, you walk guys.

To make matters worse, Sandy kept to himself. He never said nothin' to nobody. He never even cursed or argued with umps. And let me tell you, that ain't the best way to make friends on a ball club.

So back before Sandy Koufax became THE Sandy Koufax, some of the guys didn't like him.

| MOST FAMOUS JEWISH PLAYERS WHO BEGAN THEIR CAREERS BEFORE 1960 | 1ST YEAR IN MAJORS | POSITION |
|---|---|---|
| Moe Berg | 1923 | Catcher |
| Hank Greenberg | 1930 | First Base |
| Lou Boudreau | 1938 | Shortstop |
| Sandy Koufax | 1955 | Pitcher |
| Norm Sherry | 1959 | Catcher |

Not to mention, he was one of the only Jews in baseball in those days.
Some of the guys said some pretty lousy things behind his back—things
I can't repeat.

If Sandy ever heard 'em, he never let on. But maybe that's one reason he
threw too hard—to prove he was better than every one of those so-and-so's.

Then, in '57, to make a long story longer, the Dodgers moved to L.A. Yeah, that's right, some genius decided to move us to California. Can you believe that? We'd been the Brooklyn Trolley Dodgers. Now what were we dodgin'? Palm trees?

Meanwhile, the other teams were busy dodgin' . . .

. . . Sandy's pitches. In '58, he threw more wild pitches than any other guy in baseball. And after Cubs hurler Sam Jones, he walked the most batters in the National League.

If you ask me, Sandy was never gonna get any better unless he got more practice. He knew it, too. In 1960, he goes up to the general manager, "Buzzie" Bavasi, and says, "Buzzie, trade me—or let me pitch." Coulda been the most he'd said in five years!

So Buzzie listens—who knows why? He puts Sandy in the regular starting rotation with Don Drysdale and Don Newcombe. Drysdale was this big, hard-throwin' California boy. And Newcombe was one of the only black pitchers in the league. They were aces, and we all thought they'd show Sandy how to *relax*.

But it made no difference. Koufax ended the season with thirteen losses and only eight wins.

Now you know what Sandy does? He throws his uniform in the trash—the pants, the blue socks, the Number 32 jersey. Says nothin' to nobody, just leaves. *Quitsville*.

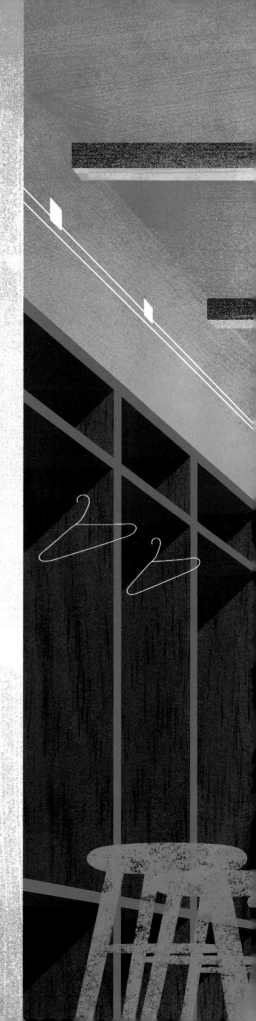

| WHEN BAD SEASONS HAPPEN TO GREAT PITCHERS | PITCHER | CAREER | CAREER WINS–LOSSES | W–L WORST SEASON |
| --- | --- | --- | --- | --- |
| | Cy Young | 1890–1911 | 511–316 | 13–21 (1906) |
| | Robin Roberts | 1948–66 | 286–245 | 10–22 (1957) |
| | Sandy Koufax | 1955–66 | 165–87 | 8–13 (1960) |
| | Steve Carlton | 1965–88 | 329–244 | 13–20 (1973) |
| | Phil Niekro | 1964–87 | 318–274 | 16–20 (1977) |

We figured he was tired of losin'. But the thing is, Sandy never struck us as a quitter. The day he left, a bunch of the guys placed bets on whether he'd be back next season. Those of us who bet he'd be back—

—well, we made a few bucks! Come spring training, who do you think shows up with a sheepish grin on his face? That's right! Kawano, the equipment manager, hands Sandy his uniform, which he'd yanked from the trash, and says, "Here, I thought you might be needin' this."

If this was a fairy tale, Sandy woulda magically been great now. But this wasn't no fairy tale, and before spring training was even over, he was pitchin' nothin' but wild stuff. Again.

Then, in this one preseason game against the Twins, he walks three guys in a row and loads the bases.

Norm Sherry, the catcher, comes out to the mound.

You can guess exactly what he's tellin' Sandy: "Kid, just put it over the plate. Let 'im hit it. We got nine guys on this team who can field."

### ONCE UPON A TIME . . .

Satchel Paige, the great Negro Leagues pitcher, would sometimes load the bases intentionally. Then he would call all his teammates except for the catcher around the pitcher's mound—and have them sit down. He would go on to strike out the next three batters—and so end the inning. The crowd loved it!

'Course, Sandy's heard this a hundred times—from Alston, from Drysdale, from other catchers—and he's always nodded. But this time, he's lookin' like he's really *heard* it. Something's different. Maybe he's standin' up a little straighter. Maybe he's turned into a statue for a coupla minutes! The bases are loaded, but Koufax don't seem the least bit nervous, he don't look worried. He don't even look like Koufax!

He goes into his windup, leans way back—
WAAAAAAY back—keepin' his eye on Sherry's mitt . . .

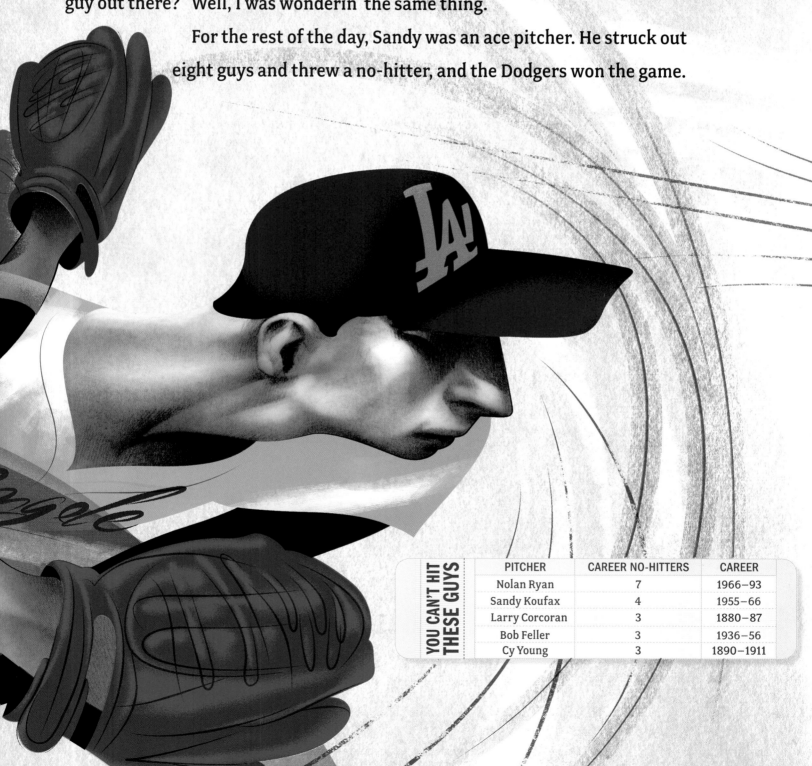

. . . and *fires* a rocket right over the plate. *Steeeee-rike!!!* I could swear it's the fastest pitch Sandy Koufax has ever thrown!

And then he strikes out the next two batters: BIM, BAM, BOOM. Down in the dugout, Alston turns to me and says, "Did you see what I just seen? Who *is* that guy out there?" Well, I was wonderin' the same thing.

For the rest of the day, Sandy was an ace pitcher. He struck out eight guys and threw a no-hitter, and the Dodgers won the game.

| YOU CAN'T HIT THESE GUYS | PITCHER | CAREER NO-HITTERS | CAREER |
|---|---|---|---|
| | Nolan Ryan | 7 | 1966−93 |
| | Sandy Koufax | 4 | 1955−66 |
| | Larry Corcoran | 3 | 1880−87 |
| | Bob Feller | 3 | 1936−56 |
| | Cy Young | 3 | 1890−1911 |

And it didn't stop there. From then on, Koufax was a strikeout *machine*. At the end of '61, Sandy had broken the National League record, with 269 strikeouts. The rest, as they say, is history.

For six *golden years*, game after game, Koufax goes to the mound and strikes out guy after guy. Game after game, he goes out and throws so hard his hat falls off.

And game after game, he throws so hard his elbow swells to the size of a grapefruit. It's so sore he's gotta stick it in a bucket of ice water when he's done pitchin'.

Game after game, he's gotta take so many painkillers he can hardly stand up. But Koufax does keep standin'—and he keeps throwin' strikes.

How do you go from being *nobody special* . . . to being THE Sandy Koufax? What happened out on the pitching mound that cold March day?

| BEST PITCHERS OF THE EARLY 1960s | | CAREER | ERA | STRIKEOUTS | NO-HITTERS | WINNING % |
|---|---|---|---|---|---|---|
| | Sandy Koufax | 1955–66 | 2.76 | 2,396 | 4 | .655 |
| | Whitey Ford | 1950–67 | 2.75 | 1,956 | 0 | .690 |
| | Bob Gibson | 1959–75 | 2.91 | 3,117 | 1 | .591 |
| | Juan Marichal | 1960–75 | 2.89 | 2,303 | 1 | .631 |
| | Don Drysdale | 1956–69 | 2.95 | 2,486 | 0 | .557 |

Nobody really knows. With Sandy, nothin' ever added up. Just when you thought you were startin' to understand him, he'd haul off and throw you a curve—like this one:

It's the first game of the 1965 World Series, which falls on a Jewish High Holy Day, and it's Sandy's turn to pitch.

But Sandy—he's nowhere near the ballpark. Why? Because if you're Jewish, you ain't supposed to work on a High Holy Day. Sandy sits out the game to show he's proud to be Jewish, and to set a good example. Just when it seems like pitchin' is all he cares about, Koufax proves everybody wrong—and becomes an even bigger hero to American Jews.

And just when he's at the peak of his game, the guy retires.

| GREATEST LAST SEASON OF A MAJOR LEAGUE PITCHER—SANDY KOUFAX, 1966 | | | | |
| --- | --- | --- | --- | --- |
| W–L | STRIKEOUTS | ERA | COMPLETE GAMES | SHUTOUTS |
| 27−9* | 317* | 1.73* | 27* | 5* |

*League Leader

You shoulda seen it when he made the announcement.
A room full of reporters' mouths fell open. It made no sense.
But if you thought about it, it made perfect sense. Sandy
had a choice: he could retire, or he could lose the use of his
left arm. And he didn't want to lose that arm.

Yessir, folks are still scratchin' their heads over Sandy. For six years, he put us all in a trance—teammates, batters, fans. In those split seconds when he arched his back and stretched his legs across the mound, his arm about to whip the ball into another world, he was like the Greek god of baseball.

| GREATEST MAJOR LEAGUE PITCHERS OF ALL TIME | | CAREER | NO-HITTERS | SHUTOUTS | WINNING % | STRIKEOUTS | ERA |
|---|---|---|---|---|---|---|---|
| | Walter Johnson | 1907–27 | 2 | 110 | .599 | 3,509 | 2.17 |
| | Christy Mathewson | 1900–16 | 2 | 79 | .665 | 2,502 | 2.13 |
| | Cy Young | 1890–1911 | 3 | 76 | .618 | 2,803 | 2.63 |
| | Pete Alexander | 1911–30 | 0 | 90 | .642 | 2,198 | 2.56 |
| | Sandy Koufax | 1955–66 | 4 | 40 | .655 | 2,396 | 2.76 |

Who was Sandy Koufax? Sandy
Koufax was a guy who finally relaxed
enough to let his body do the one thing
it was put on this earth to do. And what
a thing of beauty that was.

# GLOSSARY OF BASEBALL TERMS

**AB:** At-bat; appearance at the plate by a batter.

**American League:** One of two groups of teams in Major League Baseball.

**Assist:** The action of a player who fields the ball and throws it to an infielder for an out.

**Avg.:** Batting average; hits divided by times at bat.

**Ball:** A pitch thrown outside the strike zone, which is determined by the umpire.

**Color barrier:** The unwritten agreement among major league managers, before 1947, to bar all players of African heritage from playing on major league teams.

**Complete game:** Official credit to a pitcher who pitches from the beginning to the end of a game (usually nine innings).

**Cy Young Award:** An award given by the Baseball Writers' Association of America to the best pitcher in each league at the end of every season.

**Earned runs:** Runs given up by a pitcher (not due to any fielding errors or the pitching of any previous pitchers in a game).

**ERA:** Earned Run Average, meaning the average achieved by multiplying the earned runs given up by a pitcher times 9 (the number of innings in a regulation game), then dividing that by the number of innings pitched. The lower the ERA, the better the pitcher.

**Error:** A mistake that allows an opposing player to reach base.

**Hit:** When a batter connects with the ball and makes it safely to one of the bases.

**Jackie Robinson:** The first African American to play in the modern era of Major League Baseball, and a teammate of Sandy Koufax in 1955 and 1956.

**MVP:** Most Valuable Player—an award given by the Baseball Writers' Association of America to the top player in the National League and the American League.

**National League:** The older of the two groups of teams in Major League Baseball.

**No-hitter:** A complete game in which the pitcher allows no hits.

**Pennant race:** The contest within each league to determine which team goes to the World Series.

**Perfect game:** A no-hitter in which no walks are allowed and no errors are made by the pitcher or his teammates.

**Power hitter:** A hitter who drives in a lot of home runs and extra base hits.

**Preseason:** Games played during spring training, which do not count toward the regular season standings.

**RBI:** Runs Batted In; runs that are the result of a player's at-bat (even if the ball is caught or the player is tagged out).

**Shutout:** A complete game in which the pitcher allows no runs.

**Spring training:** The month before the regular season begins in April during which players get back in shape and play games that do not count toward the regular season standings.

**Starting rotation:** The four or five players who are used regularly as starting pitchers.

**Strike:** A ball thrown right over home plate in a very small area called the strike zone; also, a ball swung at and missed. A batter's first two fouls count as strikes.

**Strike zone:** An area over home plate that is determined by the umpire, usually stretching from just below the batter's waist to the middle of his chest. If a ball is pitched inside the strike zone, it's a strike. If it's outside, it's a ball.

**Triple crown:** A pitcher is said to hold the triple crown when he leads the league, at season's end, in three categories—wins, ERA, and strikeouts. A batter holds the triple crown when he leads the league, at season's end, in batting average, home runs, and RBIs. Both are very rare.

**Wild pitch:** A pitch thrown so far outside the strike zone that the catcher can't catch it. Runners are allowed to take as many bases as they can.

**Windup:** The pitcher's motion before each pitch.

**Winning %:** Winning percentage; determined by dividing a pitcher's wins by his total wins and losses.

**W–L:** Wins–Losses; the total wins and losses for a pitcher.

**World Series:** The best-of-seven championship series played by the National League and American League pennant winners.

## ABOUT THE STATISTICS IN THIS BOOK

Here are the online resources from which my statistics come:

www.wikipedia.org

www.baseballhalloffame.org

www.baseball-reference.com

www.baseball-almanac.com

www.baseballlibrary.com

Baseball statistics have always been and will always be interpreted differently by different fans and scholars. Often, several fans will use the same set of statistics to come up with entirely different top-ten lists. This is a very subjective and sentimental process, not an exact science. And the arguments that inevitably arise are as much a part of the baseball tradition as peanuts and Cracker Jack.

# ABOUT THE AUTHOR AND ILLUSTRATOR

**Jonah Winter** is the acclaimed author of many picture book biographies, including three previous books that feature baseball players: *Roberto Clemente, Pride of the Pittsburgh Pirates; Fair Ball!: 14 Great Stars from Baseball's Negro Leagues;* and *Béisbol!: Latino Baseball Pioneers and Legends.* His other books include *Muhammad Ali: Champion of the World; Dizzy,* which was a *Child* Magazine Best Kids' Book and an ALA-ALSC Notable Children's Book; *The 39 Apartments of Ludwig van Beethoven;* and *Frida,* a *Parents' Choice* Gold Medal winner. A poet and a painter, he lives in Pittsburgh.

**André Carrilho's** portraits grace the pages of *Porch Lies: Tales of Slicksters, Tricksters, and other Wily Characters,* by Patricia C. McKissack, and were hailed by the *Horn Book Magazine* in a starred review as "grandly melodramatic." His illustrations have also appeared in such publications as the *New York Times Book Review, Harper's Magazine,* and *Vanity Fair.* A resident of Lisbon, Mr. Carrilho makes his picture book debut with this book.

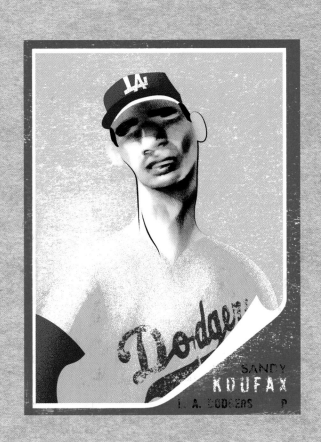